Little Mitchie

LET'S LOOK INSIDE A BEE'S HIVE

LET'S LOOK INSIDE: ANIMAL HOMES

TRACY VONDER BRINK

CREATING YOUNG NONFICTION READERS

Little Mitchie books spark curiosity and support early nonfiction reading for students in Grades 2-3. Designed to build vocabulary, support second language learners, and prepare readers for middle-grade content, each book includes helpful tips for parents and educators to build confidence and deepen understanding of the world.

TIPS FOR READING NONFICTION WITH BEGINNING READERS

Talk about Nonfiction

Begin by explaining that nonfiction books give us information that is true. The book will be organized around a specific topic or idea, and we may learn new facts through reading.

Look at the Parts

Most nonfiction books have helpful features. Our *Little Mitchie* titles include color photographs and graphic aids, a table of contents, a glossary, and an index. Share the purpose of these features with your reader.

Color Photos and Graphic Aids

A lot of information can be found by "reading" photos, charts, maps, and other graphic aids found within nonfiction texts. Help your reader learn more about the different ways information can be displayed.

Table of Contents

Located at the front of the book, this list shows the big ideas within the text and the page numbers where they can be found.

Glossary

Located at the back of the book, the glossary defines key words and phrases that are related to the topic. These words and phrases can be found in the text in colored type.

Index

Located at the back of the book, an index is an alphabetical list of topics and the page numbers where they can be found.

With a little help and guidance about reading nonfiction, you can feel good about introducing a young reader to the world of *Little Mitchie* nonfiction books.

Little Mitchie is an imprint of:

Mitchell Lane
PUBLISHERS

2001 SW 31st Avenue
Hallandale, FL 33009
mitchelllanepub.com

First Edition, 2027.

Author: Tracy Vonder Brink
Designer: Jen Bowers
Editor: Tricia Hoffman

Library of Congress Cataloging-in-Publication Data
Title: Let's Look Inside a Bee's Hive / by Tracy Vonder Brink

Description: Hallandale, FL :
Mitchell Lane Publishers, [2027]

Identifiers:
ISBN 979-8-89260-873-2 (library bound)
ISBN 979-8-89260-970-8 (eBook)

Library of Congress Control Number: 2026936347

PHOTO CREDITS
Shutterstock: cover, p.1 ©2017 Diyana Dimitrova, p.5 ©2019 Sunet Suesakunkhrit, p.6–7 ©2018 weter78, p.9 ©2019 Aleksandr Rybalko, p.10 ©2020 Kuttelvaserova Stuchelova, p.13 ©2017 Ivan Marjanovic, ©2020 Jeremy Christensen, p.14–15 ©2018 Kotomiti Okuma, p.16 ©2020 Todor Stoyanov-Raveo, p.18–19 ©2018 0 Lorenzo Bernini 0, p.19 ©2021 Ken Griffiths, p.20–21 ©2025 Serenko Natalia, p.22 ©2023 Lehrer

TABLE OF CONTENTS

Chapter One

BRILLIANT BEES

You know bees make honey in a hive. What else do they do in there? What is life like inside a beehive?

Honeybees are the only kind of bees that live in a hive. A beehive is made up of honeycombs. Each honeycomb has two layers of six-sided **cells** that honeybees make with wax.

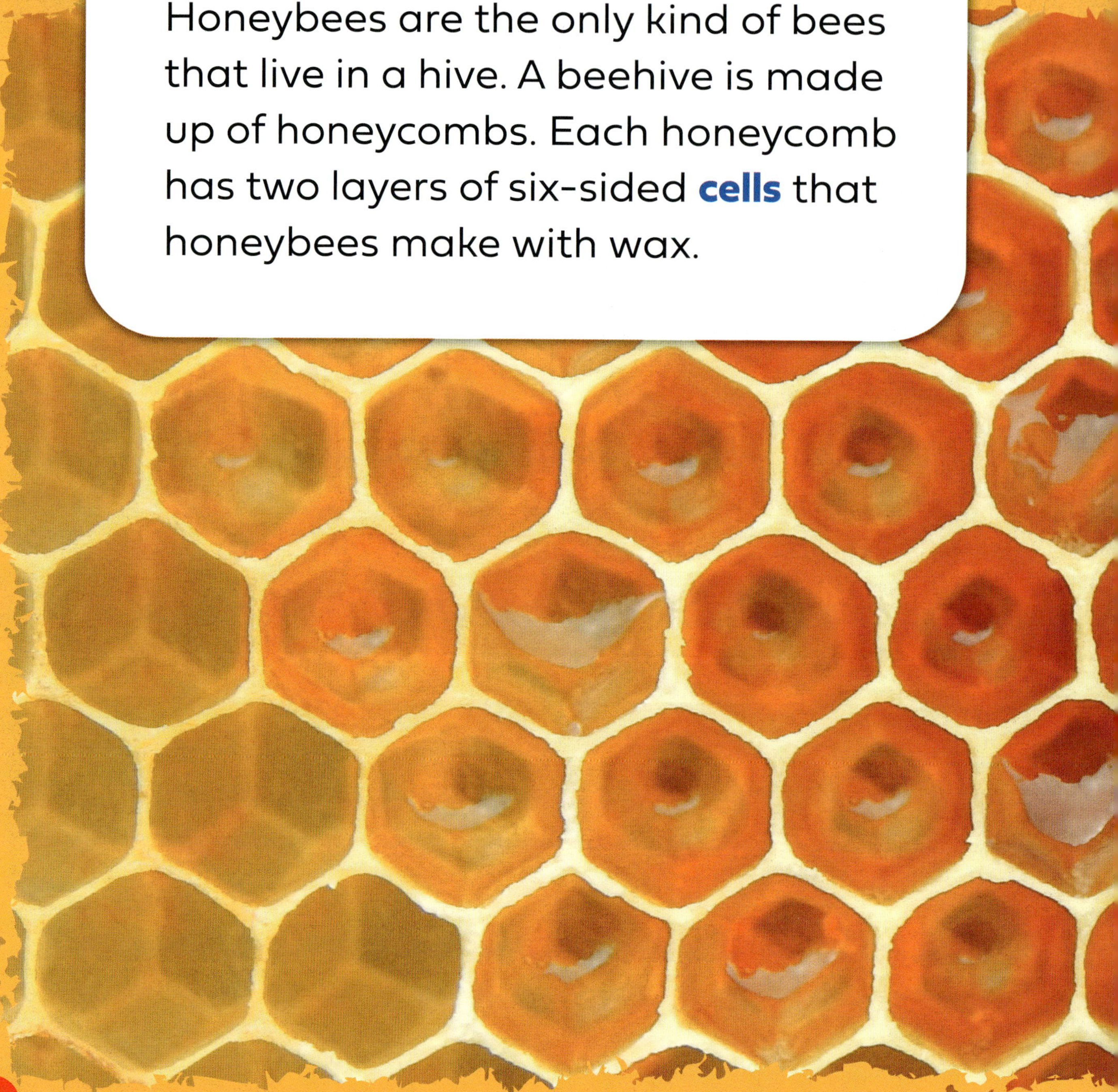

HOME SWEET HOME

Wax comes from worker bees' bodies. They chew the wax until it's soft. Then, they shape it into the honeycomb's cells.

Chapter Two

PARTS OF A BEE'S HIVE

Bees use the upper part of the honeycombs to store honey. Workers seal the honey cells with wax to keep the honey fresh. Other cells store **pollen**, which is used as food for the **larvae**.

HOME SWEET HOME

Bees use their wings like fans inside the beehive. Fanning their wings moves fresh air through the hive. It also keeps the hive cool in hot weather.

The lower part of the honeycomb has the brood cells. The queen honeybee lays her eggs there. They hatch and grow into adult bees inside the cells.

Chapter Three

LIFE INSIDE THE HIVE

Honeybees live together in a large family group called a **colony**. Each has one queen. Her job is to lay eggs. She also makes **pheromones** that other honeybees smell with their **antennae**. Her pheromones tell the workers which jobs to do. They also make the hive smell like home to the colony.

HOME SWEET HOME

A queen can lay thousands of eggs every day. She eats a special food called royal jelly that workers make and feed to her.

Worker honeybees do all the beehive's jobs. They work inside the hive for the first two weeks of their lives. Some make wax and form it into honeycombs. Others feed the queen and larvae. Some workers keep the hive clean by carrying out waste and dead bees.

HOME SWEET HOME

Worker bees are all female. Male bees, called drones, have short lives. They die after mating with a new queen.

Guard bees are workers that patrol the hive's entrance. They check bees coming back to the beehive. The guards let in bees that smell like the colony. They block any that don't. If an intruder tries to force its way in, the guards release alarm pheromones that tell the hive to attack.

Honeybees become **foragers** when they're fully grown. They leave the hive to search for **nectar** and pollen. The nectar they drink goes into a special stomach.

HOME SWEET HOME

When they get back to the hive, foragers tell the other bees where to find flowers by doing a waggle dance. The dance's movements have directions like a map. Other foragers watch the dance to learn where to go.

Back at the hive, foragers put pollen into cells. They pass the nectar to other worker bees. These worker bees take the nectar to other cells, where it slowly turns into honey.

Each honeybee is important. The whole colony works together to help each other survive. Now you know what goes on inside a beehive!

A LOOK INSIDE

GLOSSARY

antennae (an-ten-ee) feelers on the head of an insect

cells (selz) structures built by honeybees to hold honey, pollen, and their young

colony (kah-luh-nee) a large group of animals that live together

foragers (for-ij-urz) animals or people that go in search of food

larvae (lahr-vee) insects in the stage of development after they hatch

nectar (nek-tur) a sweet liquid from flowers that bees gather and make into honey

pheromones (fair-uh-mohnz) substances produced by animals that trigger a response in other animals of its kind

pollen (pah-luhn) tiny yellow grains produced by certain flower parts

FURTHER READING

Basu, Priyadarshini Chakrabarti. *Honey Bee.* Neon Squid, 2023.

Burns, Loree Griffin. *Honeybee Rescue.* Charlesbridge, 2022.

ON THE INTERNET

10 Facts About Honeybees!
www.natgeokids.com/au/discover/animals/insects/honey-bees/
National Geographic Kids shares
10 fascinating facts about honeybees.

Honeybee
https://kids.britannica.com/students/article/honeybee/637194
Learn about where honeybees are found, their
life cycle, and more with Britannica Kids.

INDEX